Making Good Cent$

Go from Penniless to Prosperous

Kelly A. Redman

Dedication

This book is dedicated to all those who have suffered or are suffering from a lack of finances. My prayer is that this book encourages you and gives you the necessary tools to get yourself on the path to financial freedom.

Contents

Acknowledgements

This book would not exist if I didn't exist, so Lord I thank you first and foremost for giving me breathe of life. Thank you also for the heart to love and serve others. I am eternally grateful.

A huge thank you to my husband Sean for allowing me the necessary quiet time away from being a wife & mother, to just be in a space to write. You are always encouraging me to do what's in my heart and I thank you for the man of God you are. You make my life pleasant and I love you dearly!

To my amazing Pastors, Bishop John & Pastor Isha Edmondson. Thank you for your integrity, transparency, and love for your "spiritual" sons & daughters. For the past 19 years, you have taught and continually teach me how to develop a true authentic relationship with God. Because of that relationship, I was able to clearly hear God's direction for writing this book.

*To my family and friends who have encouraged me, prayed for me & kept me accountable in making sure I got this book completed, **THANK YOU**! I couldn't have accomplished this without your support.*

Last, but definitely not least, to my dear friend, Pastor Joy Morgan, thank you for your "Roadmap to Destiny" class that I did not want to take (smile). That class propelled me to step out in faith and get it done. Our lives were truly destined to meet for more reasons than one! I appreciate you and have 3 words for you...IT IS FINISHED!

Preface

Are you ready to take control of your financial life, stop living paycheck to paycheck or get a fresh financial start? If so, this book is for you. It is time for you to get your financial life in order. It is time for your finances to do a 180-degree turn. This book is designed to show you how to make the necessary changes to win in life and do the things you've always dreamed of doing but it is going to take time, discipline, and self-determination. There are some things you will have to temporarily say no to for a season, but it'll be well worth it. My prayer is that this book will help you become your own financial expert.

First things first, MY story!!!! As I write this book, I am currently 48 years of age. I am a born-again Christian and proud of it. I am who I am because of my faith in the Lord, Jesus Christ. I say that not to offend anyone; however, I would not be the person I am without Him and it's an honor to acknowledge Him in all I do.

During my earlier years, I was not raised or educated properly on financial management and being a product of a single parent home, my father, who was also not properly educated on financial management, did the best he could in taking care of his family. I do not remember at any time (in elementary school, middle school or high school) learning how to properly manage money. Needless to say, for many years, I struggled to make ends meet. I got my first job while I was a senior in high school. Once I graduated high school, I continued to work. I attempted some college courses, but never really found anything of interest that I wanted to study, so off to work I went. I have had 5 jobs throughout my lifetime thus far and not much to show for it. If I would have known then what I know today about financial management, my story would have been a lot different. I would have saved more, invested more, and managed more. The good news is it's never too late. Like myself, you can start being your own financial manager today.

I don't care if you've been or are currently incarcerated, declaring or have declared bankruptcy, in debt up to your eyelids with no savings whatsoever; there is still hope. If you think your financial state is hopeless, it's not. You can always find the word "hope" in hopeless so don't give up on yourself. I'm determined to help you find a way to make things better for yourself and your family. Believe in yourself and don't focus on past mistakes, except to only learn from them and keep looking forward to a better tomorrow.

Let the journey to financial freedom begin...

Chapter 1
Developing a Winning Money Mindset

When it comes to your finances and before you can make any notable changes, you have to make up in your mind that enough is enough. You have to intentionally get tired of being where you are and make the decision to change. It's entirely up to you. No one can make the decision for you or change your mindset. So it all stems on how you think. If you can think like a winner, you'll win. At the same time, if you think like a loser, you'll lose. In his book *The Magic of Thinking Big*, David Schwartz says, "When the mind disbelieves or doubts, the mind attracts 'reasons' to support the disbelief." That's how powerful the mind is. You can find hope from hopelessness, but you have to believe that you can.

How do you develop a winning money mindset? I'm so glad you asked! You, first, have to put away any negative thinking by replacing it with positive thinking. Make a conscious decision that you are going to win with money, no longer live paycheck to paycheck and stop the cycle of repeatedly going in circles and getting absolutely nowhere. Decide to no longer live a mediocre life. No more shut off notices, evictions, late payments, bankruptcies, and borrowing money from anyone.

Winning money mindset development also requires learning from past mistakes. Not to beat yourself up, but to see where the financial trouble began. You must choose to move forward and never go back, however you must go back, from a mental standpoint, for a moment to see where your weaknesses lie. We all have weaknesses to some degree. No one is perfect and for some of you, going back might hurt a little, but it's only for a moment. Paula White has a book entitled "Deal With It: You Cannot Conquer What You Will Not Confront." That's a powerful statement; and, when it comes to our finances, we have to confront ourselves to conquer any area of financial lack that has been holding us back. Be honest with yourself and come to the realization that you are currently out of financial control.

Sometimes we stress ourselves out because we're overly concerned about our finances or lack thereof. Some of you may have made bad decisions due to the lack of money and are now dealing with the repercussions. Whatever your reason is, you have to mentally envision your way out of your financial situation and, as I stated earlier, be intentional about getting out and staying out.

If money seems to escape your bank account on a consistent basis and you find yourself penniless, make the decision that this is the absolute last time you will ever live this way. You've worked too hard and sacrificed too much time to live a mediocre life. Break the cycle of financial bondage that's been running through your family by taking control of your financial life. Be the generation in your family that creates wealth on purpose and leaves a financially healthy legacy to those coming behind you.

Lastly, developing a winning money mindset requires taking action. What decisions do you need to make to go from a negative balance to positive balance; from no savings to savings; from debt to no debt? Doing something the same year after year and expecting different results is insane. It's time to make some changes; it's time to get to work.

Mind Decluttering

Let's confront an area where you may find that you need to make some immediate adjustments. For instance, you may need to declutter your mind. Life has hit you in so many places that you cannot think straight. If that's the case, you may need to take a serious mental break. I did not say mental breakdown, I said a mental break. A mental break requires taking time for yourself every single day to declutter any negative thoughts. For instance, take 30 minutes a day, go somewhere where there's peace & quiet and just rest.

My Pastors preached a sermon back in 2018 on how to experience God's best and the definition given for resting was **"a spiritual place of confident contentment marked by a peaceful, trusting, and intimate relationship with God because of a steadfast reliance on the Lord."** That's exactly the place I want each and every one of you to be. Read the definition again and you'll find that in that place of resting, there's confidence, contentment, peace, trust and an intimate relationship with your Creator. Can't get any better than that. When you're thinking clearly, you make better decisions; you feel better about yourself; and your attitude and outlook on life is a whole lot different. Try it! If you need to, take the next 30 days and schedule time to rest. Even if you have to lock yourself in the bathroom, do what you have to do. If you need to, explain to your family (those in your household) what you're doing so they don't think you're ignoring them.

Some schools have adopted what they call "brain breaks" for kids which aides in helping students reduce stress while increasing attention and productivity. If kids need breaks, how much more do we as adults? You'll be amazed at how you'll feel in the end. You will think more clearly, and you may even get some insight into things you've been pondering.

Goal Setting

Now that you have decluttered your mind and confronted the necessary areas, it is time to start thinking about setting some goals. Think of goal setting as planning your future for the betterment of your life.

Establishing goals gives you something to look forward to in the future. Goal setting can be tedious but fun at the same time. It's imperative to set goals for your life as it helps to give you meaning in life and keeps you striving forward. From a financial perspective, setting goals assists in developing a budget whereas you are more specific in where to allocate the necessary finances to fund your goals.

There is a well-known goal setting technique called setting S.M.A.R.T. goals. This technique was developed in 1981 by George T. Doran, Arthur Miller and James Cunningham. They used the word SMART as an acronym to describe how to effectively set goals that are: Specific, Measurable, Attainable, Realistic and Timely. They developed these goals from a managerial perspective, however I'm going to break them down and make it more personable.

This requires a lot of time to think so utilize the 30-minute-a-day mental break time to think about the things you want to accomplish in life. Maybe it's a lifestyle makeover and you want the remaining years of your life to be totally different from where you are now. And that's okay. There's nothing wrong with a do over in life. Regardless of where you are now, look forward to a better future. Think of short-term and long-term goals.

Short-term goals could be 1 - 3 years from now, while long term goals could be 3 - 5 years from now.

Once you've concluded what you want to do, get some pictures that relate to each goal and place it where you will view it everyday. If you cannot find a picture, draw one. You don't have to be Picasso or Leonardo Da Vinci, just grab a piece of paper and start drawing.

Another idea would be to create a vision board where you'd take each picture and tape it to a poster board where everything is on one board so you can view all of your goals at one time. Come up with a system that works for you.

Specific Goals

In being specific about goal setting, think about the who, what, when, where and why of your future goals. What goals do you want to achieve in life and where? For example, maybe you would like to own your own restaurant. Where would you like your restaurant to be located and what would you name your restaurant? What has God put in your heart to do? Everyone on this earth is born with a purpose, find what your purpose is. For example, I have a heart to help people get out of debt and establish budgets, which is in essence why I'm writing this book. I did not know this right away. It came from personal experience of financial struggle and deciding to help others with their finances. A good place to start is by asking yourself if there's an area that bothers you; an area where you'd like to see change. Maybe God has called you to be an advocate for that area.

Next, think about who, outside of yourself, will be a part of your goals. For example, if you require employee's, get a picture of a boss with employees and place that on your vision board. A future goal of my husband's is to own a group home for troubled boys. He discovered that goal while in college earning a degree in rehabilitation education. After college, he worked for a company called Ranch Hope for Boys which continued to fuel that desire. He's not ready to pursue that goal yet; however, what he can do now is obtain as much information as possible about how to manage a group home, write a business plan, and discover "who" he will need to hire to assist in making his vision coming to pass.

Think also about why you want to accomplish certain goals. Maybe your goal is to have a soup kitchen therefore, your "why" would be to feed the homeless. Another example would be a goal of owning a 7-bedroom home in which your "why" could be to open up a bed and breakfast.

If you personally want to achieve something just for yourself, don't think of it as being selfish. If you desire a big house or luxury car or vacation home, make that a goal. Perhaps you are the first person in your family to own a home or take a luxurious vacation, do it. The only person stopping you is you! You don't need to answer to anyone about your goals.

I used to be envious of people who were able to get brand new cars, putting the first 2 miles on it. Ahh...that new car smell was Heaven to me. But I had one problem, I couldn't afford a brand-new car, nor the payments. However, I was determined to one day buy myself that brand new car and, years later, it happened. I purchased a brand-new blue Dodge Neon. It had a sunroof and I absolutely loved that car. A friend of mine, whom I joke around with all the time, said the seats were made of spandex. Those seats were sleek and smooth!! Some criticized stating they'd never purchase a brand-new car because of the drop in value once you pull it off of the lot, however, it was MY goal and My desire. Don't let anyone stop you from what you want to accomplish in life. The sky's the limit!

Financially speaking, if your goal is to be debt free, find something that pertains to debt freedom. Make a sign that says, "I'm debt free," or find scriptures that pertain to financial freedom. Don't overcomplicate the process so you won't be tempted to give up.

Lastly, when would you like to accomplish your goals? For some it may take months and others, years. It honestly depends on what the goal is, how much money (if any) it will take to accomplish the goal in question, and where you are currently in life. I will elaborate more about developing a time frame under the section entitled "timely goals." Consider that some goals may not require financial support, while others may. If financial support is needed, just sit tight and continue reading until you get to the portion where I discuss how to establish a budget, which is imperative to your life and goal setting.

Measurable Goals

Measuring your goals not only helps in determining what's needed to meet your specific goals, but it also helps you stay motivated as you're working on your goals. Measuring also requires giving yourself a timeframe of when you would like the goal to be accomplished. For instance, if you have a goal to save $1,000, how are you going to achieve that goal? Will you have a yard sale or get a 2nd job? Also, in what timeframe would you like to save $1,000? Do you want to save it in 3 months, 6 months, etc.?

Attainable Goals

In making your goals attainable you will need to think about what's required to make the goal achievable.

You may need to change unnecessary spending habits in order to save money. For instance, a few unnecessary spending habits I needed to change were going out to eat; purchasing clothes I didn't need; and buying gifts for people I really couldn't afford to buy at the time. Instead, I should have placed those funds in a savings account.

If your goal is to get debt free, you'll have to make the decision to stop financing or using credit cards. Many times people apply for credit cards as a lifeline to get them out of jams when emergencies come up. The problem is when you charge the card to its limit, never pay it off, apply for a different card, get approved and start the entire cycle of debt all over again.

Let's say you have a goal to reach a certain level within your place of employment, what do you need to do, or what skills are required to reach that level? Those are the types of questions you'd ask yourself when setting attainable goals.

Realistic Goals

Setting realistic goals requires you to ask yourself...is this the right time? Think of goals as seasons. It may not be the right season for you to set a specific time frame on a certain goal. For instance, if your goal is to own a home in 2 years, but you're currently living at home with your parents and unemployed with no savings, that goal is not realistic for you. Be assured that you're able to reach your goals in a timeframe that's attainable, but also realistic.

Timely Goals

Once you've identified that your goals are measurable, attainable, and realistic; now it's time to give it a deadline or targeted date. If you want to achieve the goal in 6 months, it's helpful to identify what you need to do today and what will be achieved half-way through the progression. This will help you stay focused and motivated.

Setting goals requires determination and dedication. When you're determined to get out of debt, you have a written plan of attack to get it done, and you have accomplished it; your whole mindset completely changes and you're armed and ready to tackle the next goal head on. You develop this winning attitude with a new perspective on life. Your values change for the better and you just become a better person overall. You'll feel a sense of urgency to keep moving forward.

Chapter 2
Let's Get to Work

If you're employed, thank God for the job that you have, whether you currently like the job or not. At least you have some type of income that hopefully takes care of your basic necessities and then some. However, if your current expenses exceed your income, find where you need to make some adjustments. You may need to work a second job, which doesn't always require leaving your home. Maybe you have a particular skill that you can utilize at home to obtain extra income. For instance, perhaps you have a niche for social media with the ability to create your own online presence to generate income. How about being a childcare provider, online teacher / tutor, medical transcriptionist? Find something that works for you, if that is indeed something you need to consider in order to earn extra income. If you find secondary employment outside of the home, make sure it's not a job that will take a toll on your health and keep you from things that are of the utmost importance to you, such as church attendance and time with your spouse and/or children.

If you're currently between jobs, submit applications as if your life depended on it, because it does. Don't settle for just any job. Calculate your expenses to determine how much you'd need to make. Once you have that amount, find a job that's equivalent to what you need to make. Notice I said NEED. In determining your needs, look at your current monthly expenses to see your needs verses wants. For example, Netflix, Hulu or Amazon Prime! Do you really need these monthly expenses in your life right now? Only you know that answer but those are just examples of subscriptions you may need to cancel. Yes, you want them, however do you currently need them? Those monthly expenses could be hindering you from having a savings account, which is far more important than catching the current episode of your favorite show. Food for thought!

There's nothing wrong with applying for jobs that exceed your basic necessities, but don't get discouraged if you don't find that job, initially. Wherever you apply, make sure it's a place that gives regular raises and as well as healthcare benefits. Some companies even offer healthcare benefits for part-time employment. Do your homework and find a place that will meet your needs.

Maybe you're already employed but have a dream to start your own business. Think about what you're passionate about. Find someone who is currently doing it, sit down with them and find out how they got started and glean from them. There's no need to compete with anyone. The late Dr. Myles Munroe said that God has put everyone on this earth to solve a problem. That problem is different for everyone. The world is waiting for your obedience! There are people who need what's inside of you. Don't think life's challenges are just for you. Keep in mind that sometimes we go through things in order to help someone else down the road. Turn every challenge into a channel for others to tune into.

If you are an entrepreneur and money is tight right now, maybe you need to consider part-time (or full-time) employment until your business gets to a place where you won't require any additional income from other sources. Maybe you need to establish more clientele, only you know what needs to be done in your particular situation.

You Are Gifted

Everyone on this planet is gifted in some area or another. Some people discover it when they're younger and others, such as myself, discover it later in life. Regardless of the timeframe, it's imperative that you find out why you were put on this planet. You are not here by accident, you are here for specific purpose and, believe it or not, God has designed you for a specific purpose.

Think about it, have you ever watched an actor just be able to act in any arena they're put in and be the best at it? When I think of an actor with such versatility, I think of Will Smith. Growing up, I used to love watching "The Fresh Prince of Bel Air." Since I liked his character, I've watched a few other movies he's been in throughout the years and have not been disappointed with his performance. He is truly gifted in the area of acting.

However, that's just one area of giftedness. There are so many other areas. Florists, massage therapists, bakers, hair stylists, teachers, authors, graphic artists, jewelers, musicians, athletes, pastors, photographers, clothing designers; the lists are endless but those are just a few other areas where people are gifted. Maybe you fall into one of those areas, maybe not, but there is something that only you can do and do well. The key is to discover what that area is. Once you find what you're truly gifted in, you'll never work a day in your life because you'll see it as a passion and not so much a job. You'll start to feel more fulfilled and you'll value what you do because it's coming from your heart.

If you find yourself trying to "find yourself," don't get discouraged. Take a personality or temperament test which may help you discover things about yourself that you've never realized. Or, ask close family members or friends who have grown up with you about what they've seen to be a consistent area in your life in which you took interest. Trust and believe that there is something you do better than anyone on this planet and work on discovering that area sooner rather than later. You'll feel so much better about yourself when you know, without a shadow of a doubt, why you are here. Too many people have lost or have taken their lives because of the simple fact of not knowing why they existed.

Once you discover your "why," begin researching that area, gaining all of the information you need to learn more about it. You may need take some classes to get additional education in that area. You may also need to find employment in that area. For example, if you have a desire to open up a coffee shop, you may need to work for one in order to get exposed to what's involved in owning your own, one day.

Until you're able to work in your area of giftedness, find a job that, again, meets (or exceeds) your daily basic necessities, while continually educating yourself on what you need to do to get to a point where you are working in your gift.

Let's also put away any extra-curricular activities that are not helping you progress towards your goals. Cancel the gym membership, especially if you're not utilizing it (or cannot afford it) and work out at home. You'll be amazed at the type of exercises you can do at home and potentially save $30 a month. Use that $30 or so that you were spending every month and put that money in a savings account to start an emergency fund! Emergencies can and will happen at some point in your life; and, having that money already put aside saves a lot of unnecessary stress.

Love "You"

Before I get into the do's and don'ts of becoming financially successful and the changes you may need to make, it's important that you first love and value yourself. For if you don't, you'll allow others to take advantage of you, especially from an employment perspective. Throughout my years, I have seen people get taken advantage of at work but, on the flip, side I've seen those who are so bold and confident within themselves that no boss could ever have the opportunity to take advantage of them. It all stems from what you think of yourself.

It reminds me of an awesome story I read about an autistic man named Michael Coyne. Because of his disabilities with not only autism, but also his diagnosis of attention deficit hyperactivity disorder (ADHD) and bipolar disorder, he was denied job after job. But that didn't stop him! He decided to take some business classes and open up his own coffee shop. You can either view that as a smack in the face to those who chose not to hire him, or a wake-up call to what was already inside him that just needed an extra nudge of disappointment to get him to move to action. Either way, I believe that, if Michael didn't love and value himself, he would have never stepped forward to take action.

A friend of mine told me another compelling story about a man named Freddie Figgers. Freddie, who was unfortunately abandoned in a dumpster at birth, fortunately was adopted by a family and later became CEO of his own company, Figgers Communication. He could have chosen to become a statistic, but instead chose to conquer his obstacles.

Those are just two examples of people who overcame the odds! There are plenty of amazing testaments of others not mentioned however the main story I want to hear about is yours. My hope and prayer is for everyone reading this book to read it, take the necessary actions, and win in life. But you have to love yourself. Learn to love you and you will never be taken advantage of another day of your life. Look in the mirror everyday and say, "I love myself some me." Do it everyday until you believe it! Do not allow any negative words to come out of your mouth as well as any negative people to be in your sphere of influence. Ladies and gentlemen, if you do those things on a consistent basis, your life (and mindset) will begin to change and you will no longer put up with mediocrity or allow others to treat you any way they want.

Loving, valuing, and believing in yourself are additives to the fire needed on the inside of you to get control of your financial life. It's not just about budgeting your money. It will help you develop an attitude of determination and motivation; that grit that'll keep you pressing forward, despite any challenges that come your way. With that kind of fire on the inside of you, nothing can stop you.

Chapter 3
Money Management

Let's delve into your financial responsibilities. The first step in managing your money is tracking your expenses. It's important to know where your money is going. The best way to do this is to track your spending for a month. I have included an example of a typical income / expense tracker form below, however you can find a variety of expense tracker forms online that may also suit you. A simple notebook will also do! If beginning with the 1st of the month makes tracking easier, then start there. Otherwise begin on whichever day you are currently on. You will need to track everything, and I mean everything, you spend for an entire month.

From a cup of coffee, to your electric bill, to going out to eat; every single penny you spend for the next month should be written down. Break down each expense into categories, such as groceries, entertainment, utilities, etc., and at months end, calculate what you've spent in each category. Doing so will help you acquire where you may be spending too much money.

Now comes the exciting or not so exciting part. Take your total income for that particular month and subtract all the expenses and you'll see whether or not you have money left over. Ladies and gentlemen, when I first did this years ago, I became saddened, not only because I may have only had about $50 or less, but also because I didn't have any additional savings to pull from if need be. If an emergency had come up, I would have had to borrow money from my father or grandmother and that's something I did not want to do. I had to make a decision to grow up and realize what I do not only affects me, but future generations behind me.

At months end, if you've subtracted your income minus expenses and have a lot of extra money left over, you're in pretty good shape, but it's time to put that money away intentionally for your future, which requires having a written budget. As you see in the sample expense tracker, the total income received thus far is $1,000 and expenses are $239 leaving $761 left to spend. Without a budget in place, outside of monthly bills still to be paid, it's way too easy to spend that extra money on unnecessary things verses putting some of it away in a savings account for future unexpected occurrences.

INCOME / EXPENSE TRACKER

INCOME

DATE	AMOUNT	DESCRIPTION	
1/3/20	$1,000.00	PAYCHECK	
TOTALS	$1,000.00		

EXPENSES

DATE	AMOUNT	DESCRIPTION	CATEGORY
1/5/20	$100.00	TITHE	CHARITABLE GIVING
1/1/20	$50.00	STARMART	GROCERIES
1/5/20	$23.00	CORNER GAS	GAS
1/10/20	$60.00	CABLE & INTERNET	UTILITES
1/12/20	$6.00	COFFEE	EATING OUT
TOTALS	$239.00		

Budgeting

The next step is creating a budget! Budgeting, in a nutshell is telling your money what to do but, unfortunately, it has been the opposite for many of us.

[24]

Your money is controlling you, putting you in financial entanglement. The only way to get untangled is to first see where the entanglement began.

One of my budget-busters was going out to eat almost every day for lunch. To combat that, instead of eating out, I had to purchase groceries and make my lunches ahead of time. I didn't like it at all, but when I think back now, I could have used a lot of that money to pay off a credit card bill I had or I could have put that money in a savings account to build up an emergency fund. Whether we like it or not, emergencies happen and having the money sitting in a savings account already, verses trying to figure out where the money is coming from, will save you from a whole lot of unnecessary stress. Think about it, if you spend $7 a day eating out for lunch for 5 days, that's $35 a week, $140 a month and $1,680 a year. That's way too much!

You may also find that a lot of your money is going to everybody else but you. Your monthly utility bills, credit card bills, medical bills, rent or mortgage payments seem to take a chunk out of your check leaving you with almost nothing to save or even spend. Ladies and gentlemen, you were not put on this earth to struggle day after day. That is no way to live! I'm sure you've heard people say "the struggle is real," as it relates to how much money someone doesn't have. Well, the struggle doesn't have to continually be real. Sitting around waiting for a miracle is not the answer; we have a part to play. *It's called management!* And please stop funding the various gambling systems, helping others get rich. Instead, use that money to create your financial future, one paycheck at a time. So let's get started....

Creating A Budget

After your initial monthly expense tracking, you should have a general idea of what you are spending on a monthly basis. Now let's put a budget plan into action. Begin by determining what your monthly income is. If your monthly income is unpredictable, meaning it varies from month to month, use the lowest monthly income you have received and budget off that amount. As your income increases, adjust your budget accordingly.

Taking a look at the sample budget provided below, the first step in budgeting is to record how much you've brought home from your paycheck which you will continue to record for each pay period. It's important to list the net income and not the gross as your gross income is before taxes, which is not money readily available to you. Listing your net income is the amount you actually have available to spend for that particular pay period. If you also received any other income for that particular period, you would record that as well.

After calculating your total income, it's now time to break down your check into categories so each dollar is accounted for. Doing this on a regular monthly basis will help you see exactly where all your money is going instead of wondering where it all went. You will also see where you need to essentially cut back or cut out certain expenses, especially if you don't have enough money left over at the end of a particular pay period.

In the sample budget, during the first pay period, the total income was $1,000. Continuing down the column for that first period, beginning with the charitable giving category, the $1,000 is broken up into the remaining categories. At the end of the 2nd sample page, the total pay period should equate to $1,000, which is what you brought home for Pay Period 1. If it equals more (or less) than $1,000, there's an area you will need to adjust.

The goal in budgeting this way is to break down every paycheck so you are not paying a bunch of bills with one check, leaving yourself empty-handed and struggling to make it until the next pay. It should also futuristically alleviate the cycle of living paycheck to paycheck.

Budgeting this way will take time and patience. Initially, during the first couple of pay periods, you may not be able to break down everything the way you'd like because it depends on when your bills are due. The best way to handle that is to list your bills in due date order, which should help you categorize your paychecks more

	Pay Period 1	Pay Period 2	Pay Period 3	Pay Period 4
Income				
Paycheck	1000.00	1000.00	1000.00	1000.00
Bonus		150.00		
Other				
Birthday Money			200.00	
Total Income	1000.00	1150.00	1200.00	1000.00
Charitable Giving				
Tithes	100.00	115.00	120.00	100.00
Offering	5.00	5.00	5.00	5.00
Savings				
Emergency Fund	120.00	120.00	120.00	120.00
Gifts / Vacation	10.00	150.00	75.00	65.00
Expenses				
Mortgage - 1,000	250.00	250.00	250.00	250.00
Utilities - 75.00	18.75	18.75	18.75	18.75
Cable / Internet - 60	15.00	15.00	15.00	15.00
Cell Phone - 80	20.00	20.00	20.00	20.00
Food				
Groceries - 500	125.00	125.00	125.00	125.00
Medical, Dental				
Insurance - 60	15.00	15.00	15.00	15.00
Copayments - 40	10.00	10.00	10.00	10.00

effectively. Within a month or so, you should hopefully be

	Pay Period 1	Pay Period 2	Pay Period 3	Pay Period 4
Transportation				
Car Payment - 150	37.50	37.50	37.50	37.50
Car Maint. - 80	20.00	20.00	20.00	20.00
Carwash / Detail-20		10.00	10.00	
Car Insurance - 175	43.75	43.75	43.75	43.75
Gas - 200	50.00	50.00	50.00	50.00
Tolls - 40	10.00	10.00	10.00	10.00
Debt				
Credit Cards				
Loans				
Entertainment				
Eating Out - 100	25.00	25.00	50.00	25.00
Sports, Hobbies		50.00		
Books / magazines	10.00		30.00	
Bowling, Movies-50	25.00		25.00	
Miscellaneous				
Gym - 26	13.00		13.00	
Hairstylist - 60	15.00	15.00	15.00	15.00
Manicure, Pedicure	25.00		35.00	
Toiletries	20.00		20.00	
Netflix, Hulu	5.00	5.00	5.00	5.00
Miscellaneous	12.00	40.00	62.00	50.00
Pay Period Totals	**1,000.00**	**1,150.00**	**1,200.00**	**1,000.00**

able to break each check down as evenly as possible. If it takes longer, it takes longer. Don't give up, keep at it until you master it. I used a simple excel spreadsheet to create this budgeting format which has worked for me for years and I hope it works for you too.

Budget Categories

Depending upon your current expenditures, you may not need to utilize every budgeting category I've listed on the sample budget. Allocate funds in each category that you're able to utilize and make sure that every single dollar is being allocated somewhere. Add categories that fit your lifestyle and don't leave any money unallocated because that is when you may end up spending it on something you don't necessarily need.

Let's take a look how to effectively set up budget categories!

Charitable Giving
Giving regularly to your local church should be first priority. As Christians, one area of charitable giving my husband and I contribute towards is tithing at our local church. Some charitable donations can also be claimed during income tax season, so make sure you include that when you do your taxes every year. For donations exceeding $250, the IRS requires you to have documentation of your contributions. Check with a tax professional and/or the IRS for rules and regulations.

Housing Expenses
These expenses would include your rent, mortgage payments, home-owners insurance, property taxes, condominium fees, maintenance fees, etc. Certain expenses, such as property taxes (if not included in your mortgage) may be on a quarterly basis, so you'd have to determine what you spend yearly on property taxes, divide that by 12 months, and set aside that amount each month. For instance, if your property taxes was $1,200 a year, divide that by 12 months and you would have to set aside $100 a month to pay that bill on time every quarter.

Regarding home ownership, if you don't have the money to purchase a home for cash, renting or taking out a mortgage would possibly be the only options, unless you plan to live with your parents or grandparents for the rest of your life. Therefore you would have to weigh your options, see what your budget allows and plan accordingly. Housing expenses can account for a major chunk of your budget and where you may find some adjustments are necessary especially in the early stages of establishing an emergency fund, which we'll discuss later.

Having your own home is a wonderful feeling; however, are you working 2 or 3 jobs to keep up with rent or mortgage payments? Did you know the Latin meaning for the word "mortgage is "death pledge"? Look it up and see for yourselves. You're ultimately pledging your life to the bank, who owns the home, until you pay it in full. Food for thought!

A great way to save in interest charges in the long run, and aide in paying your mortgage off a few years earlier, would be making biweekly mortgage payments. Biweekly payments versus monthly payments equates to 26 half-payments (13 full payments) a year which, in essence, means you are making one additional payment every year. Check with your bank or mortgage lender to find out if they have a biweekly mortgage payment plan and what it entails as some companies may charge a fee. If that's the case, do not sign up for it. You can very easily make extra payments on your own for free.

There are two different options I suggest, if you are making extra payments on your own verses using a biweekly mortgage payment plan. Option one is to pay an extra 10% of your mortgage payment each month towards the principal. For instance, if your mortgage is $1,500 a month, ten percent of that would be $150. You'd pay the $1,500 normal payment, on its due date, and then add an extra $150 towards the principle every month.

Option two would be making one additional mortgage payment every year. Using the same $1,500 mortgage payment example, you would pay the normal $1,500 monthly mortgage payment. However, you would also make another payment of $1,500, ensuring that your lender puts that payment towards the principal only. The choice is yours!

If you're struggling with making your monthly mortgage payments, maybe you need to think about downsizing until you can get yourself back above water and not financially drowning. There's absolutely nothing wrong with downsizing for a season until you can afford something bigger later. Do what you have to do, don't worry about what people say or think. Let the naysayers be naysayers. It's not about them, it's about what's best for you. Be sure to obtain some financial counseling from someone you trust before making any major decisions.

Utilities

These include your cable, water, sewer, gas, electric and telephone bills. Be aware of any utility bills that are billed quarterly, verses monthly, and save that amount on a monthly basis. If you don't have an accurate amount, use the most recent bill you have as an estimate. For example, if your quarterly water bill is $150 a quarter, that's $600 a year. Dividing $600 by 12 months equates to saving $50 a month.

If some of your utilities are taking a major chunk of your expenses, you may need to make some adjustments sooner rather than later. Maybe you need to cut the cable cord? Did she really just say that? Yes I did. Maybe not altogether, but do you really need to pay $150 or more a month for 300 channels you never watch? That's insane. My husband and I decided to cut our cable bill down by purchasing a sports package. I can do without sports, however, he graduated from Penn State on a football scholarship, so college football is in his DNA. That package saved us about $50 -$75 which, at the time, was golden. It was an adjustment because we didn't have all the channels we used to, but at the same time, it helped us in paying other expenses.

There's nothing wrong with basic cable, without all those unnecessary channels especially nowadays as people are utilizing their cell phones more. Some people only have streaming services such as Netflix, Hulu, Amazon Prime or YouTube TV, which may or may not work for you. Do some research and work with what your budget allots.

Or, if that's still too much money, how about just cutting cable altogether for a little while? I understand you just got your own place and you're so excited to finally be able to have parties and social gatherings. Oh my goodness...what will people think when they see no flatscreen TV with a DVR recorder, Alexa, and voice remote control at your fingertips? They should see someone who is intentional with saving his/her life...financially! Even if they don't, it doesn't matter. What matters is you living within your means and realizing this is just a temporary solution until you're able to get whatever you want to get, when you want to get it. So instead, have game nights with some old-fashioned board games or card games.

Getting behind in utility bills can become a hurdle in your finances. This is where shut-off notices come into play. Therefore, whatever you do, don't ignore the fact that you cannot pay them on their particular due date, call the company and work out a plan of action so it doesn't turn into debt. A simple phone call with an explanation shows you're responsible and most companies should work with you. This is not the time to ignore your bills as if they're going to go away. This is also not the time to establish a "bill drawer," where you grab them from the mailbox, stashing them away with an "out of sight, out of mind" thought process. Work out a plan to pay them off and stick to the plan.

Growing up, my grandmother used to always get on me and my siblings about leaving lights on or running water too long and, back then, I really didn't understand why. I just did what I was told. But fast forward, married with kids, I now understand the reasoning behind it. From gas and electric bills, to water and sewer bills, they all add up depending upon consumption so be mindful of your monthly usage and budget accordingly.

Food
These are your groceries, including paper goods that you normally purchase at a grocery store. If you're like me, I shop at 2 or 3 different stores, always looking for deals. One of my favorite apps to use to get cash back on select items is called "Ibotta". No matter where I shop, I always end up getting a couple of dollars back just from the app itself. Cutting coupons never goes out of style either. There are also delivery services that will do the food shopping for you and deliver it to your house.

Grocery shopping is one of my least favorite things to do so, at times, I'll order my groceries online and schedule a pickup time. And, they will put your groceries in your car for you. All you have to do is show up, park in the designated areas for pickup, and off you go. That is a very convenient service for me on days when I don't feel like food shopping, which is quite often. I haven't necessarily saved money utilizing online shopping, as the prices are about the same as if I was shopping in-store however, for me, it's the convenience of not having to walk the aisles.

Transportation
Expenses such as car payments, car insurance, gas, tolls, parking, fuel, bus or train fare, Uber, license or registration renewals, car repairs and maintenance fit

into this category. With these types of expenses, you have to be strategic on how to budget for them. Renewals, repairs and general maintenance aren't monthly expenses so saving ahead of time for these expenses is critical. By the way, car payments do not have to be a way of life for the rest of your life. We'll dive more into that later in the debt management section.

Clothing

Clothing, shoes, uniforms for school or extracurricular activities can all fit into this category. One of the best times to shop for clothes is during the end of a season. You can find some tremendous discounts during the end of summer or winter seasons. You can also find sales and coupons online via websites such as retailmenot, groupon or Raketun (formally Ebates).

Sometimes you can also find clothes in good condition at consignment shops and thrift stores. Don't ever feel embarrassed about shopping at stores that sell secondhand items.

Insurance

Insurances can include health insurance, life insurance, disability insurance, etc. If any of these insurances are deducted from your paycheck, there's no need to include it in your budget as it's already accounted for in your check.

Think of insurance as a safety net of protection for all aspects of your life. There are various types of insurances on the market which can be confusing, however do not ever purchase any type of insurance until you fully understand what the insurance is for. So much so that you can with confidence, explain it to someone else. I want you to be crystal clear about what you have, why you have it, how long you have it and how much it costs you. Before you sign on the dotted line, be sure that you can afford it.

School/Childcare

Tuition fees, books & materials, childcare, tutoring, school pictures, and field trips can all be included in this category.

Savings

Savings is a category that seems to get neglected 90% of the time because, let's face it, the money we get goes towards bills, bills and more bills. It's time to change that. Even if you have to start saving with $5, the time is now.

Entertainment / Recreation

Vacations, hobbies, book clubs, magazine subscriptions, movies, eating out, and gym memberships can all be associated within this category. This is a fun category that should not be taken for granted. We all need time to just relax and enjoy life. Not saying you can't enjoy life otherwise but doing something you love keeps you young and energized.

Medical

These expenses can include health or dental insurance deductibles, medical bills, prescriptions, and eyeglasses. Please be sure to have regular dental exams, health exams, eye exams, etc. It's important to take care of yourself. You only get one body so take great care of it.

Miscellaneous

Miscellaneous expenses equate to expenses not listed that currently are part of your everyday life. Expenses such child support payments, business expenses, computer software or apps would fit into this category. You can also include gifts, such as birthdays, Christmas, or any holidays of significance to you.

Chapter 4
Debt Management

Debt is one of my least favorite subjects to talk about, however it's what has many people financially chained up. If you don't know what debt is, financial debt, in short, is owing someone money. Debt can include current monthly payments being made to creditors, such as credit cards, mortgage lenders, student loans, car payments or even any bills that are in default.

What would your life be like if you didn't have any debt? Can you imagine actually enjoying your paycheck instead of paying every other person but yourself? Truth is you can, if you make the decision to never get into any more debt and work on paying off each creditor you owe. That is what debt management is all about.

Depending on how much income you have as well as how much debt you have accumulated, you may only be able to pay one creditor at a time. For a season, you may have to get a second job, as I mentioned previously, in order to get a handle on paying off debt.

It's so easy to swipe a credit card, but why is it that when the bill comes, it's not so easy to pay it back? If you can't pay your credit card balance in full every month, do yourself a favor and stop using credit cards. Credit card companies (as well as some other lenders) make millions of dollars off the amount of interest they charge you so do everything in your power to no longer charge anything. If carrying cash isn't the best option for you, when it comes to purchases, use a debit card which takes the money directly out of your account.

Consider this, when you're driving a car, many times all you think about is putting the key in the ignition and the pedal to the metal. You're focused with your hands on the steering wheel without a doubt in your mind that you're going to get to your destination. But then, suddenly, your vehicle goes kaput and you have no choice but to pull over and seek assistance. You lift up the hood of your car, trying to figure out the problem but to no avail and once your vehicle gets to a car repairman, they hit you with outrageous costs to fix your vehicle. You go from zero to sixty in your mind with how you're going to get the money to fix the vehicle which (mind you) is the only means of transportation that you have. That's when Mr. Credit Card speaks to your subconscious because, you know, it's the ONLY way you'll get your vehicle up and running. You don't have paid time off at work to take while your vehicle is getting fixed.

In this day and age, there are services like Uber and Lyft, modern-day taxi services which is great; however, let's say that was your lunch money for the week. Should you starve and eat oodles and noodles all week? These are the kinds of decisions people make on a regular basis when your finances are out of sorts. It's frustrating and you're stressed out not knowing what to do so what do you do? Take out good ole' faithful Mr. Credit Card, finance the repair but end up paying triple the amount in the end because you carry the balance for years. Ever been there? So have I! I don't care how old you are, you can still have freedom in your finances *if* you choose to. You may have to cut back in a lot of areas, but your diligence will pay off in the end.

Another issue is wanting something so badly that we are not patient enough to save up for it, so what do we do? Charge it. You may have every good intention on paying the balance off when the statement comes, however something always seems to come up once that statement does come and you, in turn, don't pay the balance off. Here we go again paying twice or even three times as much as the original purchase. It's an ongoing cycle of not being able to enjoy the fruit of your labor month after month.

From billboards to TV commercials or online and social media, the need to have and have now is everywhere. Buy now, pay later seems to be the norm in this society we live in. The amount of pressure to apply for credit cards is astronomical. Nowadays you can't seem to pay for your items at a retail or grocery store, without the sales associate asking if you'd like to apply for their store card. Just today, as I was checking out at Walmart, the cashier asked me if I wanted to apply for a Walmart credit card. *NO THANK YOU!*

Even at banks, whether in person or through the drive-through, you will get asked to apply for some type of credit card. Nine times out of ten, the credit card isn't the issue, its the cardholder (the person in possession of the card). If you cannot pay off your balance in full every month when your credit card statement comes in, then don't apply for one. For instance we just paid off a credit card that charged 17.99% interest on a revolving balance so even though we made a high monthly payment every month, they still charged over $100 in interest just for carrying a balance. That's just insane. Save yourself from unnecessary debt and sky-rocketed interest rates and use a debit card. And, if you don't have the money to purchase what you want, save up until you do.

Not only are credit cards an issue, but financing in general can also be an issue. Want the latest cell phone? Finance it! Always wanted a family pet but can't afford your favorite breed? Guess what's available, pet-financing. You can finance just about anything! But is financing the be-all and end-all?

I've seen those who have accumulated so much debt that they've stressed themselves out wondering how they'll ever pay it back. In those cases, declaring bankruptcy was their only option. My concerns with

[39]

declaring bankruptcy are the fees to declare it and the hit on your credit so, if you're considering bankruptcy, first look into what it entails, get some wise counseling, and be sure it's the right thing to do for you. And, whatever you do, never go back into debt after declaring bankruptcy. Declaring bankruptcy is one thing, going back into debt after declaring is just foolish. Have a plan to get out and stay out! That's why budgets are so important. As you are sticking with your budget and paying off debts, you can still save money. It may not be a lot right now, but your diligence will pay off. Just be patient!

Why is it that we aren't thinking about our future, but rather focusing on our present? When you reach retirement age, whenever that day is for you, do you want to keep working after you retire or enjoy the life as you deserve without financial strain or stress? The choice is yours but keep in mind that, every time you apply for any type of debt or financing, you are tying up future dollars. *I'll say it again...every time you apply for any type of debt, you are tying up future dollars.*

How do you manage debt? Not by paying someone to consolidate your debt, but rather by establishing a debt repayment plan, paying off one creditor at a time if that's the only option you have at this point. Or, by paying more than one creditor at a time if you're financially able to do so. Either way, be sure to include the debt repayment plan in your monthly budget. Taking a look back at the sample budget, you'll see where I purposely listed each debt in red. I did that so you'll get a visual of what debt(s) you are currently working on. You <u>do not</u> have to colorize your debt, especially if you get easily distressed from looking at them. Just be consistent and get someone to hold you accountable in making sure you're sticking to it. I don't want you to get distressed about paying your debt, but I also do not want you working the rest of your life to pay them off.

If, currently, you're only able to pay one creditor at a time, start by paying off the debt with the lowest balance first, then once that debt is paid off, utilize the money you were using to pay the previous debt for the next debt and so on, increasing the amount you pay one at a time. The goal is to be completely debt free. You may think that's not possible, but it is if you stay focused and accountable with the mindset and action of never going into any more debt.

Get into the habit of paying cash for <u>everything</u>. That doesn't mean carrying loads of cash in your pockets, as the use of a debit card would suffice. Start putting away money in a savings account. You may not be able to afford the lavishness of an expensive vacation right now but save up until you can. Choose to have an attitude of delayed self-gratification in a world where everyone wants everything now. You can do this!!

Chapter 5
Saving Your Life

One of the most important categories in a budget is a category for saving money. However, throughout my years of helping others establish budgets, savings is a category that gets neglected 90% of the time. It's not because people don't want to save, but because debt and bills have become the number one priority versus saving for your future. Unfortunately, some have become so overwhelmed with paying bills that saving money is the farthest thing from their minds and their budgets. It's time for that to change! Think of savings as a financial life preserver!

The best time to start saving money is NOW! Begin by establishing an emergency fund. Even if it's only $5 a paycheck, start with your next pay and keep increasing the amount as your budget allows. You may have to cut out unnecessary spending and use that money to fund your emergency fund. No excuses! You've heard it said excuses are like bellybuttons, everybody has one and as my husband likes to add in "and they stink." What stinks is living beneath your means and never being able to actually enjoy a paycheck.

There's a money challenge online called the "52-week money challenge," where you start with saving $1 the first week, $2 the second week and so on. Once you hit 52 weeks, you would have saved $1,378. That's a great start to an emergency fund! It doesn't matter at what week you start. You don't have to wait until the first week in January to start, if it's currently June. Start now! People that continually put savings off will never start. They will keep making excuses as to why they can't. Don't be one of those people.

Most times, emergencies happen while you're in the process of saving but don't let that discourage you. Use what money you have for the emergency and build the fund right back up. Just make sure it's a legitimate emergency and not just something unnecessarily deemed an emergency. Don't use the money for unnecessary reasons because it will only set you back.

You should continually increase your emergency fund to a point where it becomes large enough to cover at least 6 months of living expenses. Depending on your current financial state, 6 months may seem like a pretty substantial amount, but trust and believe having a nice financial cushion in the bank alleviates the stress and sleepless nights of worrying about money.

To calculate what 6 months of living expenses is for you, estimate what you normally spend every month and multiply that number by six. For instance, if you spend $1,000 a month on living expenses, $1,000 multiplied by six is $6,000.

Depending on where you bank, when you get to a substantial amount, look at a savings account that has the best interest rate, so your money is making money. For example a money market account (MMA) has a higher interest rate than a regular savings account, but also requires a higher minimum balance. Check out **www.bankrate.com** to search for different savings account options. Once you increase your emergency fund to at least 6 months of living expenses, don't stop saving. You should be saving money for the rest of your working lifetime. That's how important saving money is.

As I'm finishing up this book, we are currently facing a worldwide pandemic caused by a virus called the coronavirus. Apparently, it originated in China and is, unfortunately, spreading like wildfire and causing a lot of fear, panic, and an unfathomable amount of deaths in certain areas. A majority of businesses were forced to temporarily close as well as schools; colleges; churches;

malls; libraries; etc. With that said, many people are forced out of work with no idea of when they'll return, solely relying on unemployment to get by. Therefore, I must reiterate the importance of having 6 months of savings (or more) for situations like this current pandemic. No one knows when this will end, but to have a substantial amount of money saved already can help eliminate the fear and anxiety that comes with not having enough money.

Chapter 6
Insurance, Identity Theft Protection, Will Preparation

What exactly is insurance? Wikipedia defines insurance as a means of protection from financial loss. Think of insurance as just that: protection for you and your family. Depending upon the type of insurance, it can serve as a safety net if something were to happen that's beyond your control.

Here is a list of different types of insurances that I recommend everyone should have and a brief explanation of what they entail. Some insurances I'm listing are mandatory while others may depend on your current financial situation as well as your age. However, I believe these types of insurance are essential for living.

Auto Insurance

Auto Insurance is a contract between you and the insurance company that's designed to protect you and your family from financial losses, physical and/or bodily damage resulting from automobile accidents, etc. Auto insurance is required by law with coverage requirements differing from state to state, however here is a brief list of what auto insurance can offer:

- Coverage for vehicle repairs as a result of an automobile accident.
- Coverage for lawsuits brought up against you as a result of an accident.

- Benefits to survivors of an accident that resulted in death.
- Discounts and perks for those with good driving records.
- Coverage for theft, vandalism, and fire.

Some of these coverages are based upon your jurisdiction so make sure to do your homework to choose the best options that are affordable for you and your family.

Health Insurance

Another type of insurance that is imperative is Health Insurance. If your employer doesn't provide health insurance coverage, please look into options for acquiring your own. Even if you are currently unemployed and don't have health insurance, one website you can check out is **www.healthcare.gov** for various health care options. Do your homework to find health insurance that includes dental coverage. Health insurance should be your top priority, not only for yourself, but for your family. Taking a trip to the emergency room in an ambulance alone today is very costly. Adding on the cost of X-rays, medications, overnight stays, etc.; it can become a financial burden. However, having health insurance can at least take some, if not all, of that burden away.

Homeowners / Renter's Insurance

Homeowners and renter's insurance protects your home from property damages that may occur. However, you must do your homework to make sure you have the appropriate amount of coverage for your home as some insurance companies may only cover certain damages. For instance, if you live in an area where floods are common, you must be sure your current homeowner's insurance policy provides coverage for flood damages. The same would be true for earthquake coverage or replacement coverage in the event of fire damage. Speak with an insurance agent that you trust but be prepared ahead of time by writing down all your questions, so you are crystal clear on the type of coverage you need. Do not allow anyone to talk you into something you don't need.

Identity Theft Protection

Nowadays obtaining someone's personal information is a cinch, especially online, therefore Identity Theft Protection is another must-have. I've personally had previous email addresses hacked more than once. I've had friends whose Facebook accounts were hacked. My husband was a victim of identity theft years ago, when someone got ahold of his debit card number around Christmas time and started making purchases online. I'm sure there are many other horror stories of those who have been victims of identity theft. And, unfortunately, the turn around time to get your "name" back, if you will, can be weeks and sometimes months, depending upon the severity of the theft. Some have to get lawyers and it can be extremely messy. I don't know about you, I would not want to go about it alone. That's why this type of coverage is important!

Long-Term Care Insurance

Long term care insurance is coverage for facilities such as nursing homes, assisted living, long term in-home care, hospice, respite care, etc. This type of insurance is important, especially for those in their late 50's early 60's. Why? Because even though you may qualify for Medicare, in which certain Medicare plans cover hospital stays, nursing home care, hospice and respite care; Medicare only covers those types of facilities for a shortened period of time.

Let's face it, any type of care for yourself or a loved one can become a financial strain, especially for an extended period of time. But, pre-planning can help to alleviate that strain. Of course we need to do our part in taking care of ourselves by drinking plenty of water, eating healthy foods and doing some type of physical exercise; which are things in our control; however, what we cannot control is if any unforeseen ailment attacks our bodies.

My mother unfortunately passed away due to multiple sclerosis at the young age of 36 so you never know when something may occur. In her case, long-term care insurance would have been ideal for her at an earlier age, but my father had to pay out of pocket for her in-home care. Therefore, it's imperative to plan for the worst, even if the worst doesn't happen. At least you'll have the peace of mind in knowing that, if something does, you're already prepared.

Life Insurance

Think of life insurance as assurance that your loved one, whether it's a spouse, your children or anyone you name as a beneficiary, won't have any financial strain after you die. That's what life insurance is all about. You, as the insured, are paying for insurance to ensure that after you're gone, it can pay off any type of debt, funeral costs, etc. that's left behind. My hope is that you won't have any type of debt to leave to anyone, therefore the beneficiaries can utilize that money to invest in their future.

I can remember a time when a friend had an illness and unfortunately was unable to obtain life insurance because they already had a pre-existing condition, therefore they were denied life insurance from multiple companies. This person passed, unable to leave anything to anyone which in turn left the funeral expenses to that of their family. A very sad story but reiterates the importance of life insurance.

The best type of insurance I recommend is Term Life Insurance because it's affordable and is usually for a certain "term" or period of time. The period of time can range anywhere from 10 to 30 years. Currently, my husband and I both have 20-year term life insurance policies.

With term life insurance, you must make sure to stay current as to when your term expires so you can renew to another term prior to the expiration date. You do not want your insurance to lapse and then you unexpectedly die during that lapse of time leaving nothing to your beneficiaries.

Two people I recommend for additional information on Term Life Insurance, is Dave Ramsey at www.daveramsey.com and/or Suze Orman at www.suzeorman.com. Both have similar views about the benefits of Term Life Insurance and how it differs from other types of life insurances.

Will Preparation

Have you ever heard the saying "Get your affairs in order?" That's something a doctor would say to someone who is terminally ill and likely to die within a short period of time. What exactly are your affairs? Part of it is making sure you have a Will prepared.

A Will is a *legal document* which describes in specific detail how you want your estate and assets distributed after you die as well as any funeral wishes. Notice I said, LEGAL DOCUMENT! You cannot write your wishes down on a piece of paper and stick it in a drawer. It should be legalized in case any unforeseen issues come about such as family arguments over your whereabouts, which is unfortunately common with those who have lost a loved one without a prepared legalized will. In the absence of a will, you inevitably give permission to the state to determine how your personal belongings and finances, including any investments, get distributed. Having a will prepared gives your family peace of mind.

Think of your will as a legal love letter to your family which tells them exactly where you want everything you have left to go. For instance, if you had a substantial amount of money in a bank account, in your will you would have to specifically list how you want the money distributed. If you want it distributed to your children, spouse, aunt, uncle, grandkids, a charity, whomever; be sure you are clear-cut about it. It should be kept in a safe but accessible place so that when the time is necessary, the person in charge of your estate knows exactly where the document can be located, which is not only important to you, but also to the executor of your will.

An executor is the person responsible for making sure all your last wishes are granted. Whoever you choose as your executor should be someone you trust and believe without a shadow of a doubt will execute what you say upon your death. Some people may not want a funeral service, they may want to be cremated leaving their ashes to a certain person(s). When my grandmother passed, she stated in her will that she wanted a graveside service and her wishes were honored.

In your will should also be included to whom you choose to leave any property such as a car, home, vacation rental, boat, etc.; or if you want said property sold and the money distributed a certain way. If you have a property that still has unpaid debt, such as a mortgage, you should have in writing how you want that debt to be paid. For instance, you would put in writing that, upon your death, certain assets of your estate (provided sufficient assets are available) would take care of that mortgage.

A will is just as important, even if you don't have any financial assets or properties. Possessions such as jewelry, photographs, televisions, game consoles, bicycles, furniture; anything of sentimental value should be included in your will. You should also include who would become the legal guardian to your child(ren) in the event that both you and your spouse pass at the same time.

Furthermore, include a physician's directive (a living will), which is a legal document stating your wishes in the event you are placed in a position where you are unable to communicate your end-of-life wishes. For example, when you're hospitalized, a doctor or nurse routinely asks if you have a living will or Do Not Resuscitate (DNR) order which lets them know whether or not to perform Cardiopulmonary Resuscitation (CPR) if your heart stops. Within that, you should also include a health care power of attorney which is a person you choose to make healthcare decisions on your behalf.

Having read this section, I hope you have a better understanding of why a will is important. If you are 18 and older and don't have a will prepared, look into getting one as soon as possible. Having one will give you and your family peace of mind.

Chapter 7
Retirement

Ahh...the joys of being retired. Can you picture what that day will look like for you? Hopefully, it'll be a time of leisure, where you can relax and enjoy your life, family or whatever is important to you and NOT a time of working to pay off debts! It's the lifestyle I want for each and every one of you. The good news is it can be accomplished! The minute you think retirement is not in your future, your brain will process thoughts, and possibly actions, behind that thought.

For instance, I've witnessed those who just refuse to save money because they feel as though they can't. They get a paycheck and that paycheck is spent on everything, from bills to unnecessary items, leaving themselves penniless until the next paycheck. That is NOT the way to live. That is a financial red flag and a very dangerous place to be in. That type of person opens themselves up to unnecessary stress and anxiety. They basically live their lives borrowing money from everyone and anyone until the day they die. Don't let that person be you! That's why accountability is so important. Ecclesiastes 4:9 (NLT) says that "Two people are better off than one, for they can help each other succeed." Get on a financial plan of action, stay accountable and stick to it...period!!

The best time to start saving for retirement is in your early 20's, saving at least 10 - 15 percent of your income per year in a tax-favored retirement account. If you can start earlier, do it. If you haven't started one yet, I recommend you start one quickly. If you stick with the plan, once you hit retirement age, you'll be glad you did!

[53]

Here is a list of a few different types of retirement accounts with a brief description:

*401(k) - a corporate savings plan that you would apply for within the company where you're employed. This is a good investment to consider especially because your employer may give you "free" money through matching a percentage of your employee contributions.

*403(b) - another corporate savings plan available for public schools and certain non-profit organizations.

*the numbers and letters in these accounts refer to the Internal Revenue Service (IRS) tax code number and subsection...i.e.: 403(b) = 403 (tax code); subsection (b).

If your job doesn't offer a retirement plan, don't fret, here are other options:

IRA (Individual Retirement Arrangement) - better known as an individual retirement account or "traditional IRA", - a retirement plan that can be set up personally as long as you're earning taxable income. An IRA can be set up at your local bank, brokerage firm, mutual fund company or online. Check out **www.bankrate.com** for different options.

Roth IRA - named after the late William Roth, a former senator of Delaware, a Roth IRA is yet another taxable income earned retirement account you personally set up. The difference between an IRA and Roth IRA is the tax breaks you'll receive. There are also certain income requirements for Roth IRA's. Check the IRS website for additional requirements.

[54]

With a traditional IRA, the money you contribute is with pretax dollars, but once you begin withdrawing the money at the age of 70 1/2 (age enforced by the government), you'll get taxed on what you withdraw. With a Roth IRA, you pay taxes on the money contributed, however as long as you've had the account for 5 years and you're older than 59 1/2, you are not taxed on money you withdraw.

SEP (Simplified Employee Pension) IRA - a retirement account available for self-employed or small business owners.

TSP (Thrift Savings Plan) - a retirement account available for members of the military or government employees.

It's important to do your homework and never apply for anything you don't understand. Gain full understanding as to where your money is going, what the requirements are; tax benefits; penalties; etc.

When you begin receiving payments from Social Security, I want you to enjoy that money, not depend on it. It saddens me to see so many elderly people in dire straits who end up working at a later age just to get by. That's why it's important to take your financial life seriously. It's not a game; it's not a joke. Your financial life depends solely on you and the choices you make. *When you neglect to start saving money at an early age and neglect continuing to save throughout your "working" lifetime; it deems necessary for you to work after you retire.* Read that sentence again and really let it sink in. That's why retirement accounts are important.

If you can retire without owing anyone anything, you're in a wonderful place and the money is yours.

Yours to give to charity; bless others; take vacations; whatever your heart desires. Financially, plan well and you'll retire well, living a prosperous life.

Appendices

I've included the following forms to help you put in practice all that you've learned throughout this book. Do the work and start your journey to financial freedom!
Make Good Cents!

Mind Decluttering / Brain Break Activity

In this activity, there are two columns below. In the first, list any negative thoughts that may be hindering you from moving forward. To the right of those negative thoughts, find a positive word to replace it and choose to focus on the positive thoughts instead. Once you have finished, read and sign the declaration below as a way of telling yourself that you are making a fresh start in life, letting go of the past.

Negative Thought	vs	Positive Thought

Declaration:

As of _____,
I choose to no longer focus on any negative thoughts and I will, instead, choose to focus on positive thoughts that encourage, uplift, and propel me to do all that I have been put on this earth to accomplish.

Signature:

_____

S.M.A.R.T GOALS

Utilize the following worksheet to begin designing goals for your life. Refer back to chapter 1, if need be. Have fun with this assignment; get pictures or a vision board. This should be an exciting time for you. You are about to embark on a whole new journey. When you've accomplished each goal, celebrate it. Regardless of whether it's paying off a debt, establishing a savings account, or any other goal you've set for yourself; it doesn't matter. You've worked hard and you deserve to celebrate!

S.M.A.R.T GOALS WORKSHEET

SPECIFIC	What would you like to achieve? Answer the questions: who, what, when, why and how.	NOTES:
MEASURABLE	How will you accomplish the goal? List any tools needed? How much money will it cost?	NOTES:
ATTAINABLE	List any steps you need to take to get the goal accomplished.	NOTES:
REALISTIC	What is the timeframe you see yourself achieving the goal?	NOTES:
TIMELY	Target date set to accomplish the goal in its entirety?	NOTES:
DATE GOAL ACCOMPLISHED	When did you achieve the goal?	**NOTES:**

INCOME / EXPENSE TRACKER

Use this form to track your income and expenses for 30 days, which should help you establish your budget or tweak your current one.

INCOME / EXPENSE TRACKER

INCOME			
DATE	AMOUNT	DESCRIPTION	
TOTALS	0		

EXPENSES			
DATE	AMOUNT	DESCRIPTION	CATEGORY
TOTALS	0		

MONTHLY BUDGET FORMS

The key to your prosperity is managing your finances and managing them well. It all starts with your monthly budget. Remember a budget is telling your money what to do. No longer allow your money to manage you! I've provided a budget template for you in the following pages. However, you are welcome to create your own. Do what works for you, but please make sure you do it. It's time to reverse the curse of financial lack!

	Pay Period 1	Pay Period 2	Pay Period 3	Pay Period 4
Income				
Paycheck				
Bonus				
Other				
Total Income	0	0	0	0
Charitable Giving				
Tithes / Offering				
Savings				
Emergency Fund				
Gifts / Vacation				
Expenses				
Mortgage / Rent				
Utilities				
Cable / Internet				
Cell Phone				
Food				
Groceries				
Medical, Dental				
Insurance				
Copayments				

	Pay Period 1	Pay Period 2	Pay Period 3	Pay Period 4
Transportation				
Car Payment				
Car Maintenance				
Carwash / Detail				
Car Insurance				
Gas				
Tolls				
Debt				
Credit Cards				
Loans				
Entertainment				
Eating Out				
Sports, Hobbies				
Books / magazines				
Bowling, Movies-50				
Miscellaneous				
Gym				
Hairstylist				
Manicure, Pedicure				
Toiletries				
Netflix, Hulu				
Miscellaneous				
Pay Period Totals				

Contact Information

For information on Kelly Redman's financial planning and budgeting services; or to meet for a financial budgeting consultation, contact her at:

Instagram name - @makinggoodcents
Phone number - (856) 347-0371
Email - kredman@makinggoodcents.net